Silk Ribbon Embroidery

Gloria McKinnon

Contents

Silk Lavender Sachets 4

In My Garden 8

Lilac Time 11

Embroidered Pincushion 14

Silken Topiary 17

Poppy Pillow 20

Matrioshki Doll 24

Victorian Heart Frame 28

Silk Ribbon Embroidery Guide 31

Elegant Hat Box 33

Bridal Album 36

Ribbon Flower Bouquet 40

Silk Pillows 43

Porcelain Box 46

Editorial
Managing Editor: Judy Poulos
Contributing Editor: Gloria McKinnon

Photography: Andrew Payne, Andrew Elton
Styling: Louise Owens, Kathy Tripp, Lisa Hilton, Anne-Marie Unwin
Illustrations: Lesley Griffith

Production and Design
Production Director: Anna Maguire
Design Manager: Drew Buckmaster
Production Coordinator: Meredith Johnston
Production Artists: Petra Rode, Lulu Dougherty
Assistant Designer: Sheridan Packer
Junior Production Editor: Heather Straton

Published by J.B. Fairfax Press, an imprint of LibertyOne Media Group Pty Limited
80-82 McLachlan Ave
Rushcutters Bay, Australia 2011
A.C.N. 078 084 447
Web Address: http://www.jbfp.com.au

Formatted by J.B. Fairfax Press
Printed by Toppan Printing Co. Hong Kong

© LibertyOne Media Group Pty Limited 1999

This book is copyright. The written instructions, designs, and patterns are intended for the personal, non-commercial use of the purchaser. No part may be reproduced by any process without the written permission of the publisher.

Enquiries should be made in writing to the publisher. The information in this book is provided in good faith with no guarantee impl

Some of the material in this book has been previously published in other J.B. Fairfax Press Pty Limited publications.
JBFP 536

SILK RIBBON EMBROIDERY
ISBN 1 86343 365 1

DISTRIBUTION AND SALES
Australia: J.B. Fairfax Press
Ph: (02) 9361 6366; Fax: (02) 9360 6262
USA: Quilter's Resource Inc
2211 Nth Elston Ave, Chicago 60614
Ph: (773) 278 5695; Fax: (773) 278 1348

Silk Ribbon Embroidery

Elegant red roses, dainty forget-me-nots and cheery daffodils are all created in an instant, thanks to the charm of silk ribbon embroidery.

In recent years, embroiderers all over the world have discovered the ease and the pleasure of working with this delightful medium. There are no strands to tame and separate, and no intense concentration on the need to produce accurate, tiny stitches. Simply choose one of the fantastic range of coloured silk ribbons in the width most appropriate and begin!

There are few special stitches to learn to create a wonderful garden of flowers with your embroidery needle. The work grows so quickly, with delightful effect. Do not agonise for too long about the shape of a petal or the curl of a leaf – remember, it's the effect that's important.

Silk Lavender Sachets

EMBROIDERED BY GLORIA MCKINNON

Be ready for the gift-giving season with these delightful embroidered sachets. They feature new silk ribbon flowers that will delight you.

Materials

For all four sachets
- 15 cm x 76 cm (6 in x 30 in) of dupion silk
- 1 m (1 1/8 yd) of ribbon
- small embroidery hoop
- lavender

For the pansy sachet
- 1 m (1 1/8 yd) each of four colours of 7 mm (5/16 in) wide silk ribbon (overdyed ribbons are very suitable)
- 2 m (2 1/4 yd) of 4 mm (3/16 in) wide silk ribbon, Dark Green
- 2 m (2 1/4 yd) of 4 mm (3/16 in) wide overdyed silk ribbon, Pale Pink
- 1 m (1 1/8 yd) of 4 mm (3/16 in) wide ribbon, Black or dark contrasting colour
- 1 m (1 1/8 yd) of 4 mm (3/16 in) wide silk ribbon, Yellow, for the centres
- DMC Stranded Cotton, Dark Green
- Piecemaker tapestry needle, size 22
- Piecemaker crewel needle, size 9
- 1 m (39 in) of 5 cm (2 in) wide French organza ribbon

For the rose bowl
- 10 m (11 yd) each of 4 mm (3/16 in) wide ribbon: overdyed Pink/Lemon, Pink silk ribbon, Pale Pink silk ribbon
- 4 m (4 1/2 yd) of 4 mm (3/16 in) wide silk ribbon, Peach
- 8 m (9 yd) of 2 mm (1/16 in) wide silk ribbon, White
- 8 m (9 yd) of 4 mm (3/16 in) wide silk ribbon, Beige/Green
- DMC Stranded Cotton: Pale Green, Light Tan
- Piecemaker tapestry needle, size 22
- Piecemaker crewel needle, size 9
- 75 cm (30 in) each of two 5 cm (2 in) wide French organza ribbon

For the Canterbury bells
- 5 m (5 1/2 yd) each of 4 mm (3/16 in) wide silk ribbon: two shades of Cream, four shades of Mauve
- 1 m (1 1/8 yd) of 4 mm (3/16 in) wide silk ribbon: Plum, Green
- DMC Stranded Cotton, Dark Green
- Piecemaker tapestry needle, size 22
- Piecemaker crewel needle, size 9
- 75 cm (30 in) of 5 cm (2 in) wide French wired ribbon

For the impatiens spray
- 3 m (3 1/3 yd) of 7 mm (5/16 in) wide silk ribbon, Pink
- 5 m (5 1/2 yd) of 4 mm (3/16 in) wide silk ribbon: Pale Pink, White, Pale Blue
- 2 m (2 1/4 yd) of 4 mm (3/16 in) wide silk ribbon, Yellow
- DMC Stranded Cotton, Grey/Green
- Piecemaker tapestry needle, size 22
- Piecemaker crewel needle, size 9
- 75 cm (30 in) of 4 cm (1 1/2 in) wide antique ribbon

Method

See the Embroidery Designs on pages 6 and 7.

For all the sachets

1 Overlock or zigzag the edges of the silk, as it frays very quickly.

2 Fold the dupion silk in half to mark the base line of the sachet. Secure the fabric in the embroidery hoop. Following the stitch guide on pages 6 and 7, commence the embroidery the distance above the base line indicated for each sachet: Canterbury bells, 2.5 cm (1 in); impatiens spray, 4.5 cm (1 3/4 in); pansy 3 cm (1 1/4 in); rose bowl 1.5 cm (5/8 in).

To complete

When the embroidery is completed, fold the sachet over double with the right sides together. Stitch down the sides. Turn the sachet through to the right side, taking care to push the corners right out. Fold the top of the sachet right in until it reaches the base line. Fill your sachet with lavender, then tie a beautiful bow.

Stitch Guide

Pansy Sachet

Pansies

Using 7 mm (⁵/₁₆ in) wide silk ribbon in the tapestry needle, make six straight stitch petals as shown.

Using the Black or dark contrast silk ribbon, make four small straight stitches.

Daisies

Make five petals in ribbon stitch with a Yellow French knot centre.

Leaves are lazy daisy stitch.

Buds are straight stitches in silk ribbon with an open fly stitch in a single strand of Dark Green cotton.

Stems are Green stem stitch.

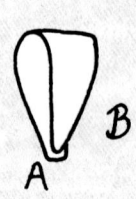 

Rose Bowl Sachet

Roses are worked in overdyed and silk ribbons in fly stitch.

Buds and leaves are ribbon stitch.

Fillers are French knots.

Bowl outline is in stem stitch, using one strand of Light Tan cotton.

Other stems and buds are in open fly stitch, using one strand of Pale Green.

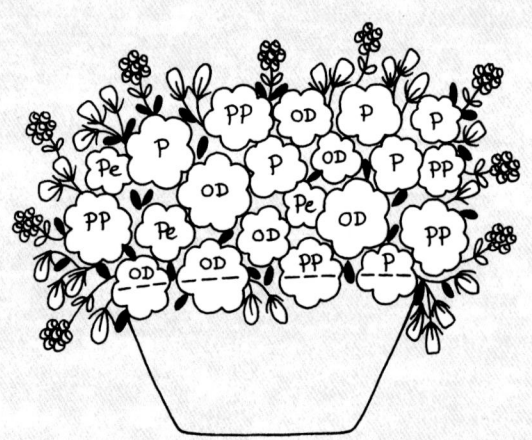

Canterbury Bells Sachet

Canterbury bells are worked in ribbon stitch, starting from 6 mm (1/4 in) from the base of the stem and working up. Overlap the bottom three or four pairs as they get smaller. Work three French knots at the top.

Stems are stem stitch using a single strand of cotton.

Leaves are lazy daisy stitch using a single strand of Dark Green cotton.

Mini-delphiniums are French knots, tapering upwards, worked in four shades of Mauve.

Daisies are ribbon stitch with a French knot centre.

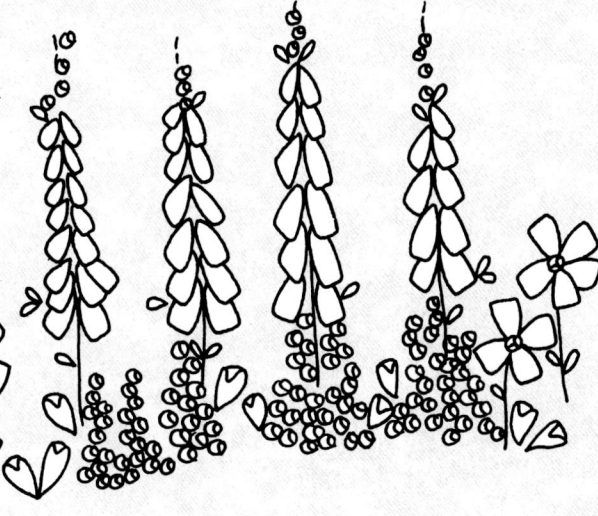

Impatiens Spray Sachet

This flower has five petals which sit out from the fabric.

Using the 7 mm (5/16 in) wide ribbon, work as for the daisy (opposite). Bring the needle up from the back at **A**, then take it to the back at **B** leaving a petal of approximately 8 mm (3/8 in) standing free. Hold that petal in your fingers when working the next petal. Work the five petals in the order shown. The centre is a Yellow colonial knot.

Stems are stem stitch in one strand of Grey/Green cotton.

Other stitches used: Fly stitch roses, ribbon stitch buds, French knot forget-me-nots, colonial knot alyssum and lazy daisy leaves.

In My Garden

MADE BY KATHY AWANDA

This little dress uses silk ribbon embroidery to its best advantage to create a special dress from a basic pattern.

Materials

- yoked dress or pinafore pattern of your choice
- sufficient fabric to make your chosen garment
- sufficient lawn interfacing for the yokes
- Piecemaker tapestry needle, size 22
- Piecemaker crewel needle, size 8
- three ceramic garden buttons
- embroidery hoop
- 1 m (1 1/8 yd) each of 4 mm (3/16 in) wide silk ribbon: Light Brown, two shades of Purple
- 3.5 m (3 3/4 yd) of 4 mm (3/16 in) wide silk ribbon, Yellow
- 2 m (2 1/4 yd) each of 4 mm (3/16 in) wide ribbon: Pale Lemon, Peach, Green, two shades of Pink
- 4 m (4 1/2 yd) of 4 mm (3/16 in) wide silk ribbon, Grey/Green
- Kanagawa silk twist thread, Green

Method

See the Embroidery Designs on page 10.

1 Mark the front yoke pattern onto a piece of the fabric and cut it out. Cut one yoke from the lawn interfacing and baste the two together securely.

2 Complete the silk ribbon embroidery on the front yoke, ensuring that the work is centred and at least 12 mm (1/2 in) above the waist seam line. It is advisable to work this embroidery using a hoop to hold your fabric square and to ensure that the interfacing does not move.

3 When the embroidery is completed, attach the buttons, then complete the garment, following the directions provided with the pattern.

Stitch Guide

Tulips

Stems are straight stitch in Green Kanagawa silk twist thread.

Leaves are ribbon stitch in Grey/Green silk ribbon.

Petals are two ribbon stitches using two shades of Pink ribbons in the needle at once, light on top and dark underneath. Work a third petal over the top of the other two. You can reverse the colours for some flowers.

  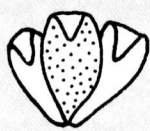

Daffodils

Petals are worked in the following steps:

two straight stitches in a Pale Lemon silk ribbon.

two more Pale Yellow straight stitches over the centre.

one straight stitch in Pale Yellow over the centre.

For the trumpet, work one ribbon stitch in a darker Yellow silk ribbon.

Stems are straight stitch in Green Kanagawa silk twist.

Leaves are straight stitch in Green silk ribbon with the ribbon twisted.

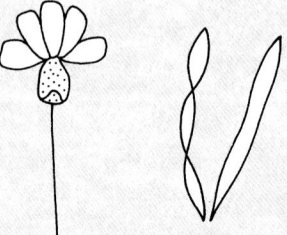

Violets

For the petals, work five small straight stitches in Purple silk ribbon with a Yellow French knot in the centre.

Large leaves are buttonhole stitch and the small leaves are ribbon stitch, both in Grey/Green silk ribbon.

Lilac Time

STITCHED BY GLORIA MCKINNON

These pretty boxes come already covered and ready for you to embroider a special lid.

Materials

- large Sudberry House moiré box
- 25 cm x 30 cm (10 in x 12 in) of matching moiré fabric
- 5 m (5½ yd) each of 4 mm (³/₁₆ in) wide silk ribbon: Purple, Deep Lilac, Variegated Lilac
- Piecemakers tapestry needle, size 22
- DMC Stranded Cotton, three shades of Green
- Piecemakers crewel needle, size 8
- three pieces of Pellon, each 25 cm x 30 cm (10 in x 12 in)
- water-soluble marker pen
- craft glue
- template plastic

Method

See the Embroidery Design on page 12.

Embroidery

1 Using the marker pen, carefully transfer the embroidery design to the centre of the moiré fabric.

2 Embroider the leaves in stem stitch, using one strand of Green, using a different Green for each leaf. Keep the stitches small to make smooth, even lines.

3 Embroider the lilac flowers in ribbon stitch (Fig. 1), working four petals for each flower. The flowers should be quite small and even, so make each stitch 3 mm (⅛ in) long. Begin with the main flower at the base, then the intermediate flowers and finally the dark smaller flowers.

Assembling

1 Trace the cardboard lid piece onto the template plastic and cut out the shape. Lay the plastic over the embroidery so that it is centred. Trace around the shape. Trim the fabric so that it extends 2.5 cm (1 in) beyond the traced outline.

2 Cut two pieces of Pellon the same size as the template, and another piece that is 2 cm (¾ in) larger all around.

3 Centre the larger piece of Pellon on the cardboard and glue it in place. Clip into the overhanging edges, turn them to the other side and glue them in place. Lay the other two pieces of Pellon on top of the first one.

4 Sew a gathering stitch around the embroidery, approximately 1 cm (⅜ in) from the edge of the fabric. Place the embroidery on the Pellon-covered piece and pull up the gathering so that the embroidery sits firmly. Lace the back with double threads for strength. Make sure there are no puckers and the edge is quite smooth.

5 Glue the embroidered piece to the pre-made box lid.

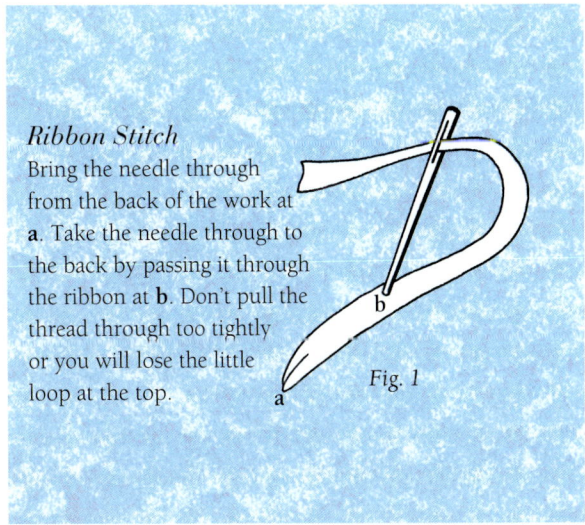

Ribbon Stitch
Bring the needle through from the back of the work at **a**. Take the needle through to the back by passing it through the ribbon at **b**. Don't pull the thread through too tightly or you will lose the little loop at the top.

Fig. 1

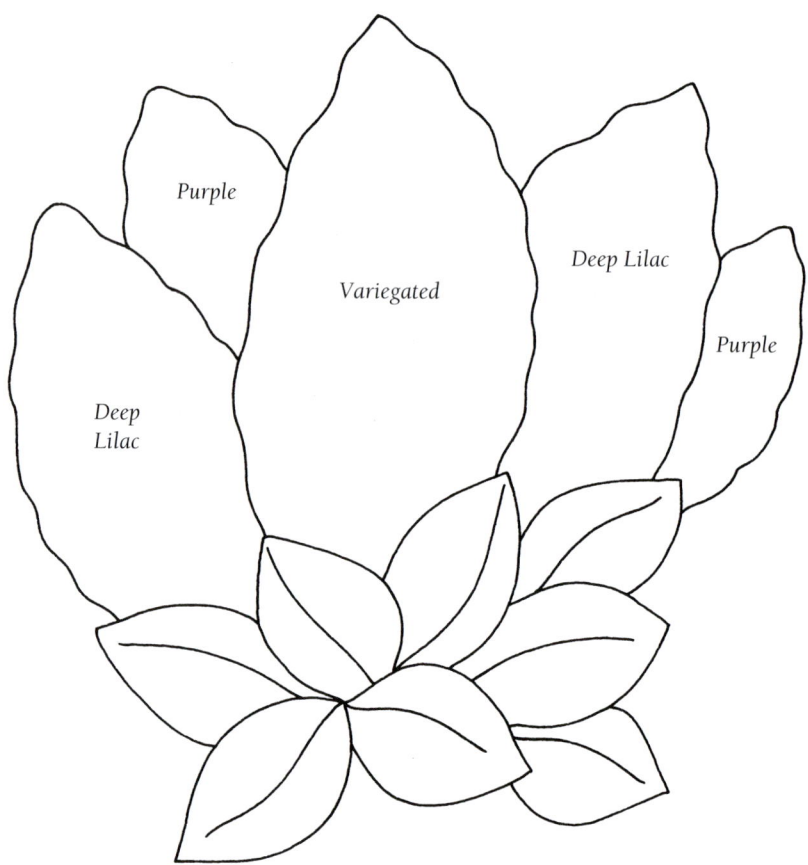

Embroidered Pin Cushion

STITCHED BY GLORIA MCKINNON

This beautiful combination of dupion silk, wonderful lace and silk ribbon embroidery makes a very stylish accessory.

Materials

- Sudsberry House Shaker box pin cushion
- 12 cm x 18 cm (5½ in x 7 in) of bottle green dupion silk
- 18 cm (7 in) of 2 cm (¾ in) wide needlerun insertion lace
- 1.5 m (1⅔ yd) of 4 mm (³⁄₁₆ in) wide silk ribbon, Deep Pink
- 1 m (1⅛ yd) each of 4 mm (³⁄₁₆ in) wide silk ribbon: Burgundy, Deep Green, Blue, Yellow
- Piecemakers tapestry needle, size 24
- Piecemakers crewel needle, size 9
- ordinary sewing thread, Cream
- DMC Perle cotton, No. 5, Burgundy
- embroidery hoop
- 450 craft glue

Method

See the Embroidery Design and Stitch Guide on page 16.

1 Using the Cream sewing thread, stitch the lace down the centre of the dupion silk.

2 Embroider the flowers over the lace, following the embroidery design and stitch guide.

3 When the embroidery is completed, make up the pin cushion, following the instructions supplied with the kit. Make sure the fabric sits quite smoothly all around the edges and it is glued firmly into the base.

Twisted cord

1 Cut four lengths of Perle cotton, each 2 m (2¼ yd) long. Tie them together with a knot at one end and secure this end to a chair back, door knob or something similar.

2 Holding the other end, twist the cord clockwise until it is so tight that it will twist against itself. You can test this as you go.

3 Fold the cord in half, allowing it to twist evenly. Cut the end that is secured to the chair or door and knot all the ends together.

4 Glue the twisted cord neatly around the pin cushion, tucking the ends under.

Stitch Guide

Fly stitch rose
Using the Deep Pink or the Burgundy silk ribbon, begin with a fly stitch, then add two more spokes. Build up the rose by weaving the ribbon tightly three times around the spokes, clockwise, then another two times loosely.

Daisy

Using Yellow silk ribbon, work five lazy daisy stitches. Work a Burgundy French knot for the centre.

Forget-me-not

Work six Blue French knots around a Yellow French knot centre.

Rose bud

Work a ribbon stitch bud to match the rose. For the stem and fly stitch, use a length of silk thread from the edge of the fabric.

Leaf

Work detached chain stitches in Deep Green.

Embroidery Design

Silken Topiary

EMBROIDERED BY GLORIA MCKINNON

Bring the garden indoors with this beautiful silk embroidery on a dainty pillow.

Materials

- 35 cm (13½ in) of raw silk
- 10 m (11 yd) of 4 mm (³/₁₆ in) wide overdyed silk ribbons in your chosen colours
- 1 m (1⅛ yd) of 4 mm (³/₁₆ in) wide silk ribbon, Green
- 3 m (3¼ yd) of 4 mm (³/₁₆ in) silk ribbon, Dusky Pink
- stranded cotton: Green, and a colour to match the silk ribbon selected for the bow
- small embroidery hoop
- 1.4 m (1½ yd) of Liberty print cotton
- 3 m (3¼ yd) of lace edging
- 3 m (3¼ yd) of fine piping cord
- ordinary sewing cotton
- polyester fibre fill
- Piecemakers tapestry needles, size 24

Method

Preparation

1 Cut a piece of raw silk 28 cm x 35 cm (11 in x 13½ in). Overlock or zigzag the edges to prevent fraying. If the piece is too small to secure into the embroidery hoop, baste pieces of calico to the edges.

2 Mark, with lines of basting, the outline of the topiary, stem and pot in the centre of the fabric.

Embroidery

1 Embroider five chain stitch ribbon roses in the circle (Fig. 1). Start in the centre with a colonial knot, then work as usual for a detached chain stitch, but instead of taking the needle down at **A**, cross it over and take it to the back at **B**. Your next twisted chain stitch will start inside the first at **C** (Fig. 2). Continue around the centre in this way until the rose is a suitable size.

2 Fill the entire circle area around the roses with tightly packed French knots in various-coloured silk ribbons. Around the very edge, stitch small Green ribbon stitch leaves, in groups of three.

3 For the stem, bring the Green silk ribbon from the back at the base of the circle. Now, twist the ribbon down the length of the stem, holding the twists in place with French knots worked in embroidery cotton. Take the ribbon to the back at the stem base.

For the pot

1 Starting at the centre top, bring the ribbon from the back at **A** and lay it vertically down the length of the pot, taking it to the back at **B**. Bring it up again at **C**, right beside **B**, and take it to the back at **D** (Fig. 3).

2 Continue in this way to cover one side of the pot. Begin again beside the centre line to cover the other side of the pot. Ensure that all the ribbons lie flat.

3 Once all the vertical ribbons are in place, weave the horizontal ribbons from right to left, then from left to right, working from the top to the bottom.

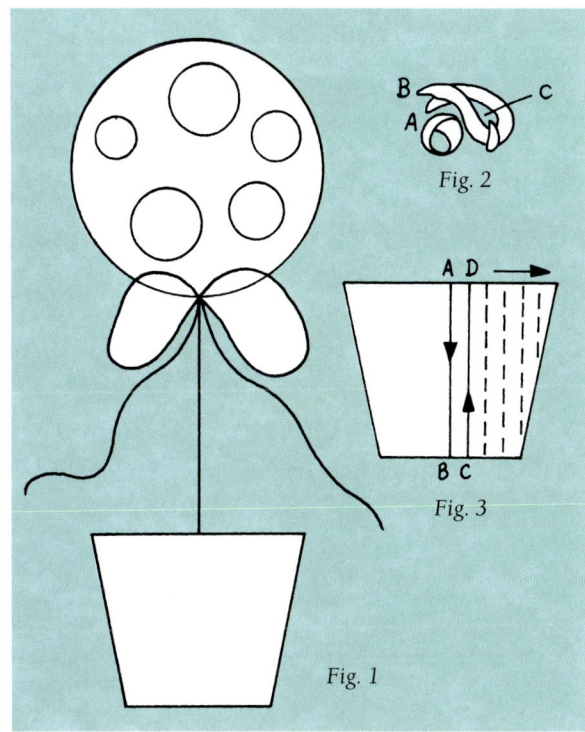

Fig. 1

Fig. 2

Fig. 3

4 Work a row of chain stitch across the top and bottom of the pot.

5 When the pot is completed, embroider a scattering of French knots around the pot and a few ribbon stitch leaves.

For the bow
Shape the ribbon to form a bow. Attach the bow with French knots in a cotton which matches the silk ribbon.

Making up

1 Trim the piece of embroidered silk to be 23 cm x 25 cm (9 in x 10 in).

2 Cut two 2.5 cm (1 in) wide strips down the length of the Liberty fabric, then join them to make one long strip and use it to cover the piping cord. Stitch the piping cord around the embroidered piece, with the raw edges matching, using the zipper foot on the sewing machine to allow you to sew as close as possible to the cord. Clip into the seam allowance of the piping to allow it to curve around the corners.

3 Cut four pieces of Liberty fabric, each 9 cm x 46 cm (3½ in x 18 in). Sew one to each side of the embroidered panel, matching centres and stitching in the piping stitching line. Stitch up to each corner, but do not stitch through it into the seam allowance.

4 Fold and press the mitres at each corner. Hand-sew or machine-sew the mitres into place. Trim away any excess fabric.

5 Stitch piping around the edge of the borders, on the right side with the raw edges matching.

6 From the remaining fabric, cut a back, 2.5 cm (1 in) larger than the front.

7 Cut two 15 cm (6 in) wide strips down the length of the fabric. Join them to make a loop. Press the strip over double with the wrong sides facing. Pin the lace to the loop with the straight edge of the lace matching the raw edges of the loop. Gather this edge with two rows of gathering. Pull up the gathering carefully to fit around the embroidered piece, adjusting the gathers so they are even.

8 Pin the frill to the pillow front and stitch it in place in the piping stitching line, placing a little extra fullness at the corners.

9 Place the pillow back over the front with the right sides together and the raw edges matching. Stitch around the outside edge, taking care not to catch the ruffle in the stitching and leaving an opening for turning. Turn the pillow to the right side, stuff softly and close the opening by hand.

Poppy Pillow

DESIGNED BY GLORIA MCKINNON, STITCHED BY LYN SYLVESTER

These wonderful California poppies add another dimension to silk ribbon embroidery. The overdyed silk bias ribbon is soft and pliable and is ideal for this project.

Materials

- 1.2 m (1$^{1}/_{3}$ yd) of silk fabric
- 3.5 m (3$^{3}/_{4}$ yd) of 12 mm ($^{1}/_{2}$ in) wide overdyed silk bias ribbon
- Kanagawa silk twist, Light Olive Green
- DMC Stranded Cotton to match the silk ribbon
- Piecemakers crewel needle, size 9
- 23 cm x 30 cm (9 in x 12 in) of tulle or net
- 40 cm (16 in) square of Pellon
- waterproof laundry marker
- water-soluble marker pen
- polyester fibre fill

Method

See the Pattern on the Pull Out Pattern Sheet and the Embroidery Design on page 23.

Preparation

1 Cut a 40 cm (16 in) square from the silk fabric. Because the silk frays so readily, it is a good idea to overlock or zigzag the edges. Baste the Pellon to the back of the silk square.

2 Trace the design from the pattern sheet onto the tulle or net using the laundry marker, and allow it to dry completely.

3 Centre the tracing over the square of silk and mark the design onto the fabric using the water-soluble marker. This will leave a series of dots marked on the fabric.

Note: It is always advisable to test the water-soluble marker on a scrap of fabric before you begin.

Embroidery

For the stems and leaves

Complete the embroidery of the stems and leaves before working the flowers. Work the stems and leaf veins in stem stitch, using a small even stitch. Work the leaves in straight stitch, following the outlines to give the shape (Fig. 1). Use the Kanagawa silk twist for all the stems and leaves.

For buds 1 and 2

1 Cut approximately 12 mm ($^{1}/_{2}$ in) of silk ribbon and fold it in half lengthwise (Fig. 2).

2 Fold the ribbon over to form a bud (Fig. 3) then, using one strand of cotton, sew a gathering thread across the base (Fig. 4). Pull up the thread to gather the ribbon, tie off the ends and fold the raw edges to the back. Appliqué the bud into position.

For bud 3

1. Cut approximately 2.5 cm (1 in) of silk ribbon. Fold the ends to the back to make a loop (Fig. 5). Sew a gathering thread across the base. Pull up the thread to gather the ribbon and tie off the ends.

2. Turn the ribbon through so that the gathering is on the inside. Stitch the bud into place. Fix the top of the bud in place with a tiny stitch.

For poppies 1 and 2

1. Cut the remaining ribbon into three lengths. Using a single strand of cotton, sew a gathering thread along one long edge of the ribbon. As you form the poppies, ease the ribbon along this edge as you go.

2. For the first petal, starting at point **A**, attach the ribbon to the fabric with a small stitch. To begin forming the poppy, fold back approximately 6 mm ($1/4$ in) of ribbon and stitch so that the ruffled edge lies along the line **A - B**. When you are approaching point **B**, cut off the ribbon and fold back approximately 6 mm ($1/4$ in) of ribbon as before. Stitch right to point **B**.

3. Start the second petal just behind the first one, bringing it around to finish at point **C** (beginning and ending with a fold as before). Now, make the third petal so that it comes in front of the first one.

4. Still using the one strand of cotton, catch the outer edges of these petals approximately 3 mm ($1/8$ in) from the outer edge at approximately 12 mm ($1/2$ in) intervals, ensuring that each small stitch is hidden among the gathers. This will hold the petals on the fabric. You will need to take one row of gathered ribbon across in front of these three petals starting at the base of the third petal and crossing to point **C**.

5. Embroider the stamens in pistol stitch and French knots. Work the stamens onto the base of the last petal.

6. Work the fourth petal in two parts. Attach a row of gathered ribbon, starting at point **D** and working back towards point **C** (with the frill lying across the stamens). Do not cut the ribbon, but work back towards point **D** with the frill lying away from the centre. When the petal is attached, turn it up toward the centre and catch it as before to hold the petal in position.

For poppy 3

Work as for poppies 1 and 2, except that the fifth petal will lie away from the centre, then a sixth petal will lie towards the centre over the fifth one (as for the last petal on the other flowers). Follow the arrows on the pattern for the direction of the petals.

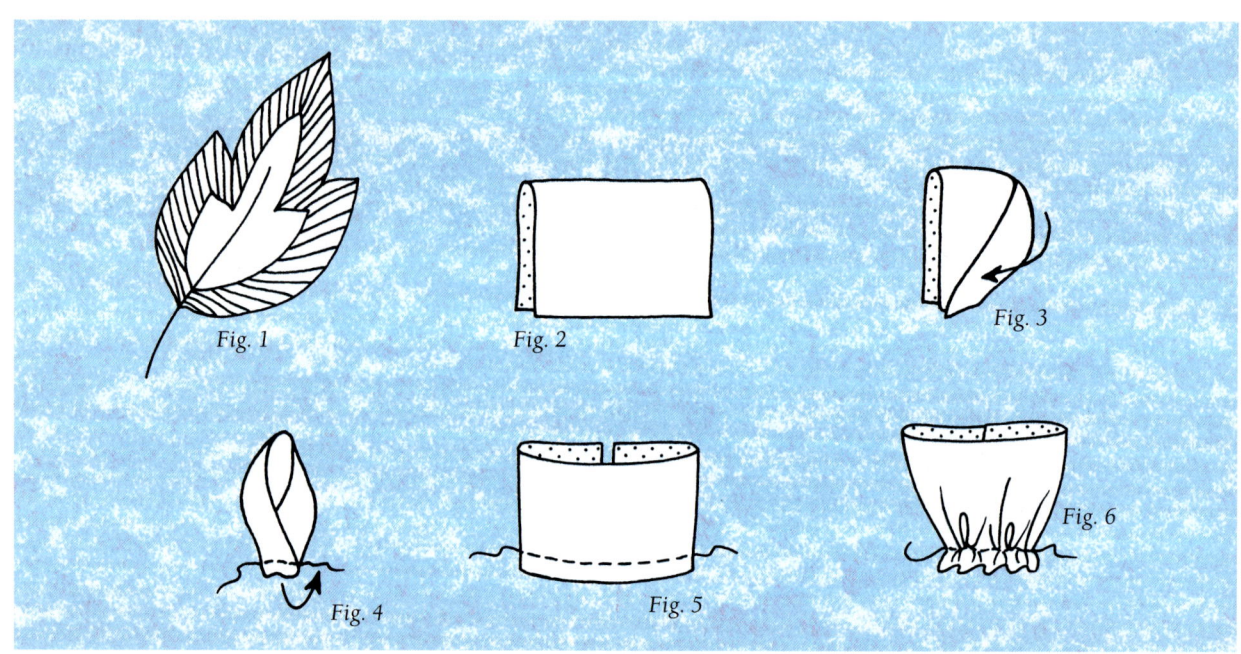

Fig. 1   Fig. 2   Fig. 3
Fig. 4   Fig. 5   Fig. 6

Finishing

1. Cut four 20 cm (8 in) wide strips across the width of the silk fabric. With the right sides together, stitch the ends to make a loop. Fold the loop over double with the wrong sides together. Overlock or zigzag the raw edges together to reduce fraying. Mark the loop into quarters.

2. Stitch two rows of gathering around the loop and pull up the gathering to fit the pillow. Pin the ruffle to the pillow, matching the quarter marks to the corners, with the frill facing the centre and making sure that all the seams are hidden within the gathers. Stitch the ruffle into place.

3. Cut a 40 cm (16 in) square of silk for the back. Pin the pillow back and front together, with the right sides facing and the ruffle pointing towards the centre. Stitch around three sides and 3 cm (1¼ in) onto the fourth side at each end, taking care not to catch the ruffle into the seam. Turn the pillow to the right side through the opening, making sure that the corners are square. Fill the pillow and slipstitch the opening closed.

Matrioshki Doll

MADE BY MARIA KIRK, ENGLAND

This exquisite embroidered doll was inspired by traditional Russian dolls and would be a delight to own or give as a gift.

Materials

- 23 cm x 25.5 cm (9 in x 10 in) piece of black heavy silk fabric
- 15 cm x 17.5 cm (6 in x 7 in) piece of wine-coloured silk fabric
- two 4 cm (1½ in) diameter cardboard circles
- 4 m (4½ yd) of 4 mm (3/16 in) wide silk ribbon: Rich Purple, Green, Burgundy, Antique Gold
- spool of thread, Gold
- 2 m (2¼ yd) of fine gold cord
- wadding
- viscose or mohair for the hair
- Doll's House 1/12 scale doll's head on a shoulder plate
- craft glue
- strong thread
- tacky craft glue (optional)

Method

The skirt

See the Pattern and the Embroidery Design on page 27.

1 Fold over and baste the edges of the black fabric to prevent them fraying. Finger-press the fabric in half, then in half again. Baste along the fold lines to mark the fabric into quarters.

2 Using one of the lines of basting as a guide for the centre front of the skirt, embroider the skirt design, following the embroidery design on the pattern.

3 Using the strong thread and running stitch, gather the edge of the circle. Pull up the gathering until the fabric forms a ball, then stuff it firmly with the wadding until you have a nice rounded shape.

4 Attach the head to the top of the skirt ball, slipping the shoulders inside and making sure the face is lined up level with the embroidery. Tie off the gathering threads to close the ball.

For the headscarf

1 Using a running stitch, sew the two scarf pieces together around the curved edge. Turn the scarf to the right side. Carefully turn in the raw straight edges. Whipstitch the edges together neatly.

2 Following the embroidery design, work the embroidery around the scarf. Work the edging by couching the gold cord down with the Gold thread.

Finishing

1 Glue the hair neatly onto the head with a little glue, taking care not to place it too far down over the forehead. Take the excess hair around to the back of the head and glue it down neatly.

2 Making sure the top embroidery on the headscarf is centred, dab a little glue on the top of the head and carefully stick down the headscarf. Hold it in place with pins, while you adjust it to your liking, then sew it in place. Carefully stitch the ends of the headscarf together under the chin, using a little glue if necessary to hold it, then, as neatly as possible, sew the headscarf to the skirt. If you wish, you can use a tacky fabric glue to help hold the scarf.

3 Cover the two cardboard discs with the black fabric by turning the fabric edge over the card and gluing it in place. Glue both card discs together, then whipstitch them together. Pin the gold cord around the edge, then couch it in place with the Gold thread. Finally, glue the disc to the base of the skirt ball, making sure the doll is well balanced.

Note: To make your doll a little special, try adding a few drops of potpourri oil to the stuffing of the skirt – but take care not to get any on the fabric – or you can use her as a special pin or needle cushion.

KEY

- ∴ *Detached chain, Rich Purple*
- ✳ *Ribbon stitch, Green*
- ◖◗ *Spider's web roses, Burgundy*
- ◊ *French knots, Antique Gold*
- ≋ *Bullion stitch, Gold*

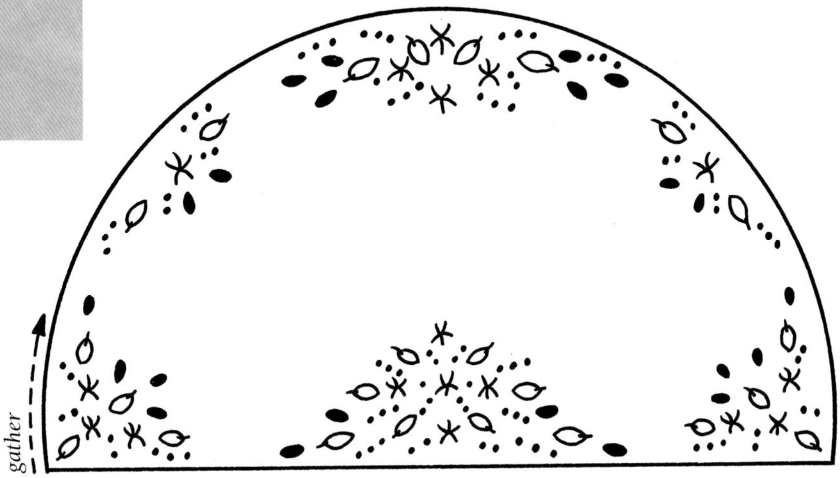

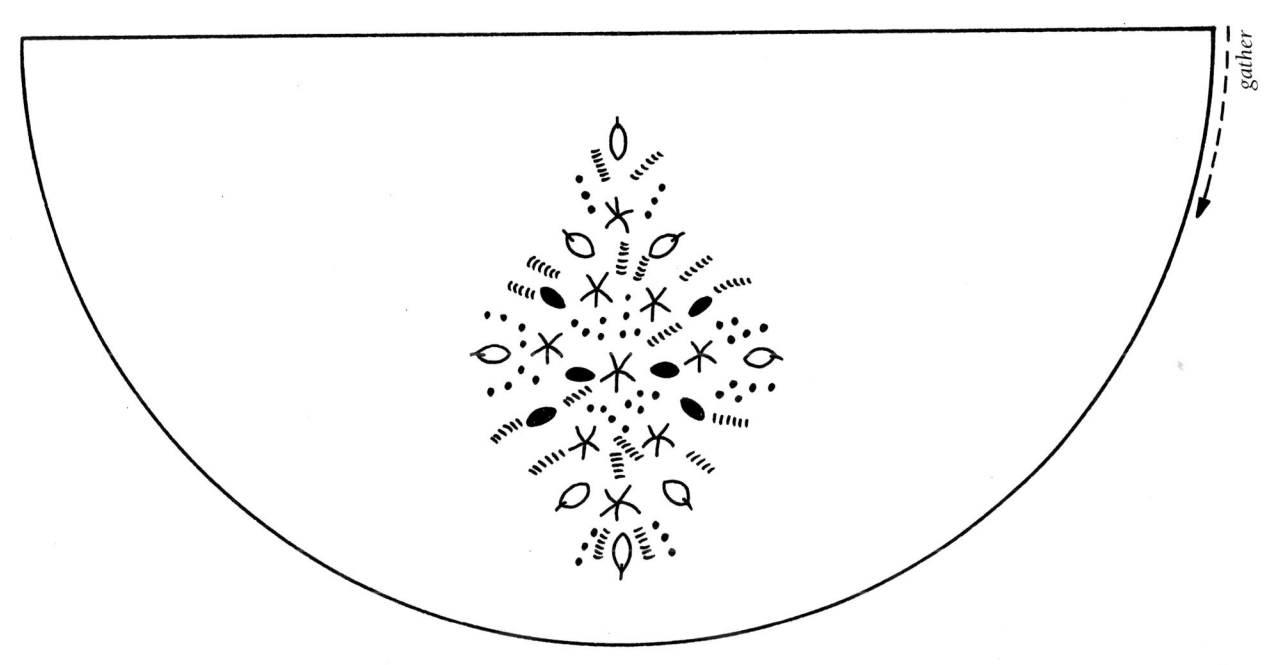

Victorian Heart Frame

DESIGNED AND STITCHED BY JUDITH BAKER MONTANO, COLORADO

Frame those special memories in a beautiful heart-shaped frame, festooned with a spray of silk ribbon flowers. This nostalgic picture frame is a wonderful introduction to the art of silk ribbon embroidery.

Note: This frame and three other kits produced by Quilters' Resource in the United States are available from Anne's Glory Box.

Materials

- 23 cm x 92 cm (9 in x 36 in) of cream moiré fabric
- 18 cm x 54 cm (7 in x 21 in) of fleece
- 20 cm (8 in) of each of three 1 cm (3/8 in) wide satin ribbons
- 76 cm (30 in) of each of two fancy cords
- 16.5 cm (6½ in) art board picture frame with a prop
- 76 cm (30 in) each of fourteen 4 mm (3/16 in) wide silk ribbons
- 61 cm (24 in) of silk buttonhole twist thread
- beads, including small pearl beads
- 1 m (1⅛ yd) of Nymo thread
- Perle cotton
- beading needles
- chenille needle, size 22
- sharps needle, size 10
- water-soluble marker pen
- tracing paper
- pencil
- 15 cm (6 in) embroidery hoop
- spray adhesive
- craft glue
- scalpel or knife

Method

See the Patterns on the Pull Out Pattern Sheet.

1. Trace the floral design and the heart pattern onto the moiré, using the marker pen. Do not cut out the fabric yet. Secure the fabric into the hoop with the traced pattern facing upwards.

2. Make the concertina flowers first and sew them into place with the Nymo thread.

3. Following the ribbon embroidery guide on pages 31-32, work the remaining flowers. Use the buttonhole twist thread for the feather stitch. Highlight the embroidery with beads and small pearls.

Assembling

1. Remove the embroidery from the hoop. Mark 12 mm (½ in) beyond the solid pattern line on both the outer and inner edges. These are your cutting lines. Cut out the embroidered frame front. Erase any visible marks from the back with a wet cloth and cold water. Set the piece aside.

2. On the moiré fabric, mark two frame backs (without the inner heart opening) and two props. Cut them out 12 mm (½ in) beyond the solid pattern lines.

3. On the fleece, mark two frame fronts (with the heart opening) on the solid line and one 12 mm (½ in) beyond the solid line. Cut the hearts out on the marked lines.

4. Glue the three fleece hearts to the frame front, placing the larger fleece heart on top. This ensures a smooth edge when you fold the fleece to the back. Spray the top fleece with the adhesive and glue the finished embroidered front to the padded heart front. Clip along the inside and outside edges, stopping the scissors at the board's edge.

5. Fold the fabric edges around to the back and glue them in place.

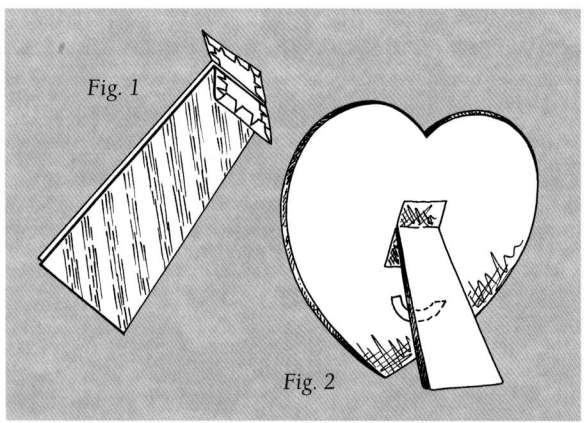

Fig. 1

Fig. 2

6 For the frame back, spray one side of a board back with adhesive. Lay the wrong side of the moiré backing onto the sprayed area. Clip the moiré edges, then fold the fabric around to the back and stick it down.

7 Repeat step 3 to make another back. Glue the two backs firmly together, with the wrong sides facing, then weight them with books until the glue is dry.

8 Score each prop on the dotted line with the back of a knife or scalpel. Cover the unscored sides with moiré fabric as for the backs. Glue them together, leaving 2.5 cm (1 in) ends above the scoring free of glue (Fig. 1). Press the prop under books until the glue is dry.

9 Glue the front and back of the frame together along the bottom and sides, leaving the top portion free to insert a picture.

10 Decide on the angle of tilt of the frame, then glue the prop to the back at the appropriate angle. To ensure the prop stays put, measure the distance between the prop and the heart back, then cut this length from the remaining satin ribbon. Glue the ribbon from the prop to the back of the frame (Fig. 2).

11 Apply glue lightly along the frame's joined edges, then cover the edges with the twisted cords. Tie them in a knot on the side and let them hang in a tassel form.

Judith Baker Montano's Tips
for Silk Ribbon Embroidery

Template plastic
Use template plastic to make a window template for all the patterns.

Threading the ribbon
Remember, silk ribbon is delicate and will fray on the edges. Use a short length 30-40 cm (12-16 in).

Needle eye lock
Thread the ribbon through the eye of the needle. Pierce one end of the ribbon, directly in the centre and 6 mm (¼ in) from the end with the point of the needle. Pull the long end of the ribbon and lock it into the eye of the needle.

Soft knot
Make the needle eye lock, then grasp the end of the ribbon and form a circle with the end of the ribbon and the point of the needle (**A**). Pierce the end of the ribbon with a short running stitch (**B**). Pull the needle and ribbon through the running stitch to form a soft knot.

Ribbon manipulation
Learn to use the ribbon properly. If it is pulled too tight or it twists too much, it will just look like a heavy thread. Use your free thumb to hold the ribbon flat against the fabric. Most stitches depend on the ribbon being flat. Keep the thumb in place while you stitch and tighten the ribbon over the thumb. This will remove any twists. A large needle or a knitting stitch holder can be used instead of your thumb.

Adjusting the ribbon
Sometimes the ribbon will fold up on itself as it passes through the fabric, and it has to be adjusted so the full width of the ribbon shows. Hold the ribbon flat under your free thumb and slide the needle under the ribbon, then gently slide the needle back and forth, from the thumb to the needle hole in the fabric.

Correct needles
Above all, use a chenille needle. Remember the heavier the fabric, the larger the eye of the needle you should use.

Silk Ribbon Embroidery Guide

Bullion-tipped lazy daisy stitch
A most effective variation of the simple lazy daisy stitch where a bullion stitch replaces the anchor stitch. The petal or leaf is changed, depending on the length of the lazy daisy stitch and the bullion stitch. Keep the ribbon flat and taut. Come up from the bottom at **A** and make a loop. Go down again at **A**. Come up at **B** (like a basic lazy daisy). Grasp the ribbon in your free hand and loop it under the point of the needle. Keep the ribbon flat. Wrap the ribbon around the needle two or three times. Hold the bullion twists in place with your thumb and pull the needle through. Hold the bullion knot firmly on the fabric and in line with the twists. Anchor the bullion knot by going down through the fabric again.

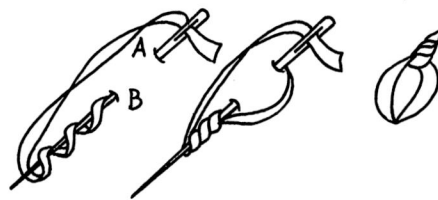

Colonial knot
This is a lovely little knot that sits up and has a little dimple in the centre. Come up from the bottom at **A**. Form a backwards **C** with the ribbon. Insert the needle under the ribbon at the top of the backwards **C**. Now, grasp the ribbon and form a loop over and under the needle. This forms a figure 8 (**B**). Hold the needle vertically and pull the knot firmly around the needle. Insert the needle as close to the original hole (but not into it) as possible (**C**). Always hold the ribbon in place until the needle is pulled to the back. This forms a neat colonial knot.

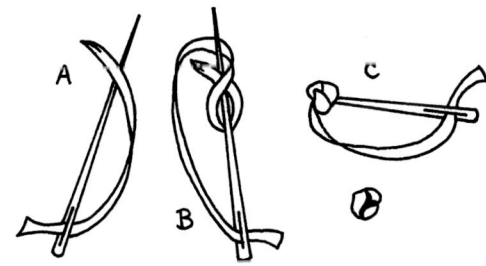

Concertina rose
Thread the needle, using thread that matches the ribbon, and knot the end. Use a 20 cm (8 in) length of ribbon. Fold the ribbon at a right angle in the centre (**A**). Fold the horizontal section of ribbon over and to the left (**B**). Bring the ribbon up on the bottom and fold it up and over (**C**). The folds will take on a square look (**D**). Keep folding from right side to top to left side to bottom until the ribbon is used up. Grasp the two ends in one hand and let go of the folded ribbon. It will spring up in accordion folds. Hold the two ends in one hand and pull gently down on one ribbon (it doesn't matter which one) until a rose is formed. With the knotted thread, go down through the top and up again. Do this two or three times. Finish on the bottom and wrap the base tightly, make a slip knot, and cut the thread, leaving a 15.5 cm (6 in) tail to sew down later. Cut the two ends of the ribbon as close to the base as possible.

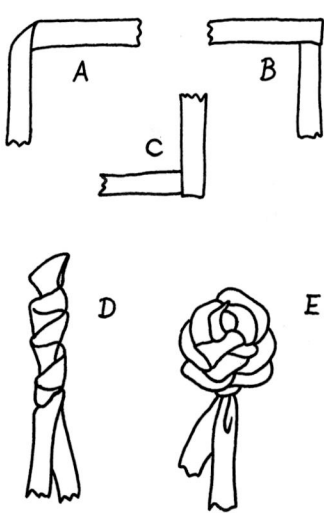

Curved whip stitch

Keep the ribbon flat. Make a straight stitch the desired length, **A** to **B**. Bring the needle up again at **A**. Wrap the straight stitch two or three times, working toward **B** and keeping the ribbon flat. Repeat the wraps working toward **A**. Anchor the last wrap stitch by passing the needle to the back. Crowd the stitch so it will curve.

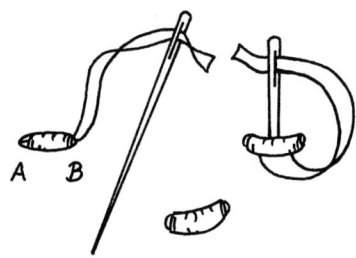

Feather stitch

This is a vertical stitch and alternates from right to left. It is worked from top to bottom. Begin with a single stitch. Come up at **A** and go down at **B**. Come up in the centre, below **A** and **B** at **C**. The secret is to always put the needle in at **B** straight across from where the thread came out at **A**.

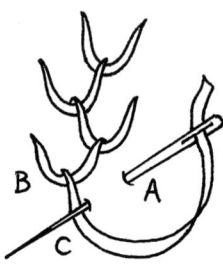

French knot

Bring the needle up and circle the ribbon twice around the needle. Hold the ribbon off to one side as you insert the needle in the fabric, as close to the starting point as possible. Hold the knot in place until the needle is pulled through.

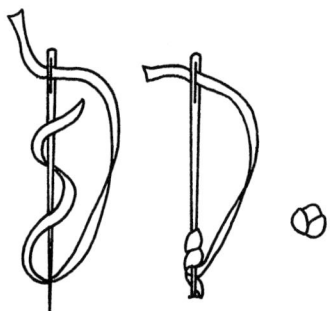

Japanese ribbon stitch

Come up under the fabric at point **A**. Make sure the ribbon lies flat by running the needle under the ribbon. Lay the ribbon flat on the fabric and pierce the ribbon in the centre at point **B**. Gently pull the needle through to the back. The ribbon will curl at the tip, but the whole effect will be lost if the ribbon is pulled too tightly. Petals and leaves can be varied by length, and by adjusting the tension of the ribbon before piercing, it can be quite loose.

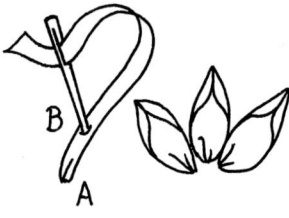

Lazy daisy stitch

This stitch is a free-floating chain stitch. Bring the needle up from the back and hold the ribbon flat with your thumb (**A**). Insert the needle at the starting point so the ribbon forms a loop. Bring the needle out a short distance away. The needle passes over the ribbon. Take a small anchor stitch at the top of the loop. Length of the stitch and the anchor can be varied.

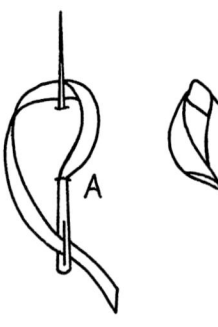

Montano knot

Designed for the effect and not for the technique! This glorified French knot is loose and effective for filling in and for floral sprays. Depending on the size desired, it varies from one to six twists. Bring the needle up from the back and circle the ribbon around the needle one to six times. Hold the ribbon very loosely and do not hold the ribbon off to one side. Insert the needle into the fabric as close to the starting point as possible. Do not pull tight; let the knot remain loose and flowery.

Plume stitch

Worked from top to bottom. Come up at **A** and go down 3 mm (1/8 in) away at **B**. Keep the ribbon flat at all times. Make a loop and control it with a round toothpick. Hold the loop in place with your thumb and come up at **C** piercing the fabric and ribbon. Form another loop. Continue down until the plume is finished.

Elegant Hatbox

COVERED BY JANELLE MESTON, DECORATED BY FAY KING

Even if you don't own a single hat, you will love this beautiful hatbox. The hatbox is from a kit by Helen Norton and is made up and covered following the instructions provided with the kit.

Materials

For covering
- large hatbox kit
- 1.5 m (1²/₃ yd) of fabric
- 1.5 m (1²/₃ yd) of lining fabric
- 1 m (1¹/₈ yd) Pellon fleece
- 450 glue
- spray adhesive
- thirty clothes pegs
- packaging tape
- Piecemaker crewel needle, size 5
- sewing thread to match the fabric

For the roses
- 2 m (2¹/₄ yd) each of three colours of 4-5 cm (1¹/₂-2 in) wide French wired ribbon
- 2 m (2¹/₄ yd) each of two colours of 5 cm (2 in) wide sheer ribbon
- 2 m (2¹/₄ yd) of 5 cm (2 in) wide wired ribbon, Green
- Piecemaker crewel needle, size 8
- sewing thread to match the ribbons

Method

For the roses

1 Cut a 50 cm (19⁵/₈ in) length of sheer ribbon and the same length of wired ribbon. Place the sheer ribbon against the wired ribbon and treat them as a single piece.

2 Fold down the end of the ribbon so that the sheer ribbon is on the inside (Fig. 1).

3 Fold the ribbon in half again in the direction of the arrow, then fold it in half again (Figs 2 and 3).

4 Using a hat pin or something similar, roll the ribbon in the direction of the arrow to form the centre of the rose (Fig. 4). Remove the hat pin but keep a very firm hold on the base of the rose with your thumb and forefinger.

5 Fold the loose part of the ribbon away from you, folding it diagonally as shown in figure 5. Continue to roll up the ribbon, folding it away from you each time you use up the folded edge. Continue until all the ribbon is used up. Putting in a few stitches as you go may be helpful. When you come to the end of the ribbon, run a row of gathering across the end (Fig. 6). Pull up the gathering and secure the end (Fig. 7). Make six more roses, using various combinations of wired and sheer ribbons.

For the rosebuds

1 Cut a 15 cm (6 in) length of wired ribbon. Tie a knot in the centre and hold both ends together below the knot. Adjust the shape of the knot.

2 Cut a 12 cm (4³/₄ in) length of Green wired ribbon. Fold over one edge, then wrap the ribbon around the knot, like a shawl. Wind thread around the base of the rosebud to secure the ribbon.

For the leaves

1 Cut 15 cm (6 in) of Green wired ribbon. Pull up the wire at one edge of the ribbon to gather it (Fig. 8).

2 Fold the ribbon so that the gathered edges are together. Pull and shape the wire at the closed edge to give it a point like the end of a leaf. Wrap the loose wire around the other end of the leaf to secure it (Fig. 9).

Finishing

Place the roses, rosebuds and leaves into a pleasing arrangement on the hatbox lid. Glue them into place.

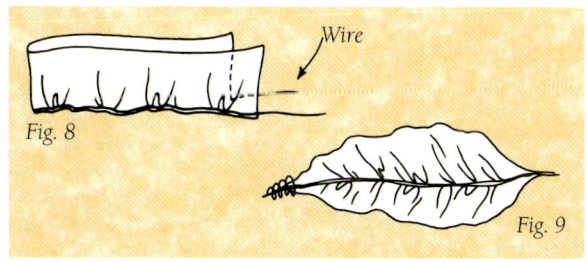

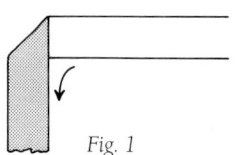

Fig. 1

Fold down the end of the ribbon.

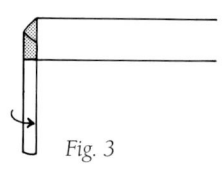

Fig. 3

Fold the same end again.

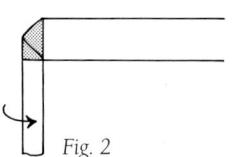

Fig. 2

Fold the same end again.

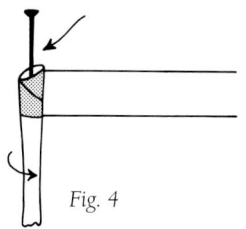

Fig. 4

To complete the centre fold once more. A pin can make this easier to do.

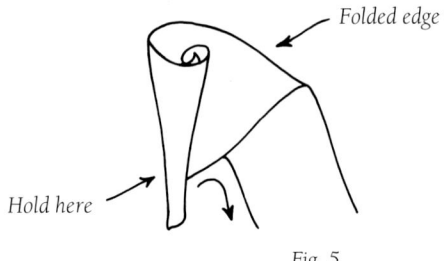

Folded edge

Hold here

Fig. 5

Holding the base of the rose firmly, turn it slowly and at the same time, fold the ribbon away from the centre.

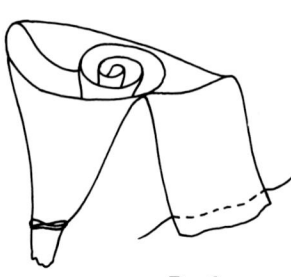

Fig. 6

Continue to roll and fold the ribbon until the desired size is reached. Secure the base with a few stitches. Run a gathering thread across the free end.

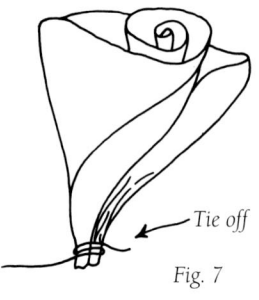

Tie off

Fig. 7

Pull off the gathering and secure around the base of the rose.

Bridal Album

EMBROIDERED BY GLORIA MCKINNON, COVERED BY JANELLE MESTON

This photograph album has been lovingly embroidered and covered to hold beautiful memories of a bride's special day.

Materials

- 75 cm (30 in) of pink Swiss Nelona batiste
- 10 m (11 yd) each of 4 mm ($3/16$ in) wide silk ribbon: Pink, Pale Pink
- cotton thread, Pale Pink
- DMC Stranded Cotton: Ecru, Pale Green
- bread dough cherub
- Piecemakers tapestry needle, size 22
- Piecemakers crewel needle, size 8
- glass-headed pin
- 40 cm (16 in) of Rayfelt
- 40 cm (16 in) of Pellon
- 450 Craft Glue
- spray adhesive
- refillable photograph album with screws
- sheet of cardboard, white (ivory-board weight)
- 15 cm (6 in) embroidery hoop
- HB pencil
- Fray Stoppa
- 1 m ($1 1/8$ yd) of 5 cm (2 in) wide pink organza ribbon

Method

See the Embroidery Design on page 39.

Weaving

1 Measure the front cover of the album and cut a piece of batiste that is 10 cm (4 in) wider and 10 cm (4 in) longer. Using the pencil, trace the heart shape onto the centre of the fabric.

2 Secure the fabric in the embroidery hoop so that the entire heart shape is showing. The woven ribbon pattern on the heart is worked with the Pink ribbon travelling vertically and the Pale Pink ribbon travelling horizontally. Using the Pink ribbon and starting at the left-hand side of the heart, lay straight stitches of ribbon side by side so that each one is exactly beside the preceding one (Fig. 1). Stitch, alternating the direction of the stitches, until the entire heart is covered.

3 Using the Pale Pink ribbon and beginning at the base of the heart, bring the ribbon through from the back and begin to weave under and over the Pink ribbon. As each row is completed, take the ribbon through to the back and bring it out again one ribbon width away, ready to begin the next row of weaving. Continue in this way until the entire heart is woven, taking care that the ribbons lie flat and smooth. Remove the batiste from the embroidery hoop.

4 Cut a piece of Rayfelt the same size as the batiste and baste it to the back of the batiste, around the edges. Return the piece to the embroidery hoop.

5 Using a long piece of the Pink ribbon, bring the ribbon through from the back at the dip in the top of the heart. Thread a second needle with a length of Pink ribbon and using this ribbon work a French knot over the first ribbon, approximately 6 mm ($1/4$ in) away from the point of exit. Allow the first ribbon to twist once, then secure it with another French knot, approximately 12 mm ($1/2$ in) from the previous one (Fig. 2). Continue in this way around the outline of the heart, taking the ribbon to the back when you return to the beginning.

Ribbon roses

1 Thread a crewel needle with the cotton thread. These roses are best wound around a pin and stitched to secure them as you go. Fold down one end of the Pink ribbon and lay the pin into position as shown in figure 3.

2 Roll the ribbon around the pin several times for the centre of the rose. Take a few stitches through the base with the cotton thread to secure the centre.

3 Fold the ribbon back and continue to wind the rose in the same direction (Fig. 4). As you pass the folded section, stitch through the base again, then make another fold. Keep folding, winding and stitching until your rose is the desired size, then wrap the thread securely around the base to secure it. Leave a long length of thread to attach the rose to the heart. Trim the ribbon ends. Make approximately twenty-eight roses in Pink and twenty-eight in Pale Pink.

4. Decide where you will place the cherub, then plan the arrangement of roses around the heart. You can refer to the embroidery design as a guide. Attach the roses, using the thread attached to each one.

5. Using two strands of Ecru cotton and a crewel needle, work French knots around the roses.

6. Using one strand of Green cotton and a crewel needle, work small detached chain stitches for the leaves.

7. Using a length of the Pink silk ribbon, tie a bow and attach it to the dip at the top of the heart. Sew three roses over the knot of the bow, then embroider French knots and leaves around the roses.

8. Using the craft glue, attach the cherub to the heart, so that the roses nestle around it.

Cutting the cover

1. Take apart your refillable photo album so that you have three pieces ready to cover – the front and back covers and the centre binding.

2. Cut a second piece of batiste the same size as the embroidered piece to cover the back of the album.

3. Cut two pieces of batiste the same size as the centre binding without a turning allowance.

4. Cut two pieces of cardboard the same size as the inside of the covers and two pieces of batiste the same size plus 2.5 cm (1 in) turning allowance on each side.

5. Trim the Rayfelt attached to the back of the embroidered piece so that it sits neatly on the cover. Cut a second piece of Rayfelt to sit neatly on top of the back cover.

Assembling

1. Using the spray adhesive, evenly spray the outside of the front and back covers as far as the fold (the attachment area). Place the Rayfelt onto the area you have sprayed, smoothing any lumps from the centre out to the edge.

2. Carefully centre the embroidered design on the front cover, taking care not to catch the batiste underneath. Glue the raw edges of the batiste and Rayfelt to the inside of the front cover.

3. Turn the allowance on the outer edge over onto the inside of the cover. Glue the edge in place, using the craft glue. When you glue down the opposite edge, nearest the binding, you must take into account the fold in the attachment area. Position the attachment area as if the album were closed before gluing the fabric over the edge. Take the edge of this fabric over and underneath the cover and glue it down on the edge of the fold line B (Fig. 5). Turn the fabric over twice so that no raw edges are visible.

4. With the point of a pair of scissors, carefully make two holes in the fabric for the screws and finish the holes with fray stopper.

5. Fold over and glue the raw edges of the top and bottom. Fold the turning allowance over twice so that no raw edges are visible and mitre the corners which fall on the edge of the first side.

6. Cut two pieces of Pellon the same size as the lining cardboard. Using a light spray of glue, attach the Pellon to the cardboard. Smooth out any lumps from the centre to the edge. Trim the Pellon to the edge of the cardboard. Place the Pellon face down on the batiste and glue the raw edges of the batiste over the cardboard, keeping the batiste taut and mitring the corners.

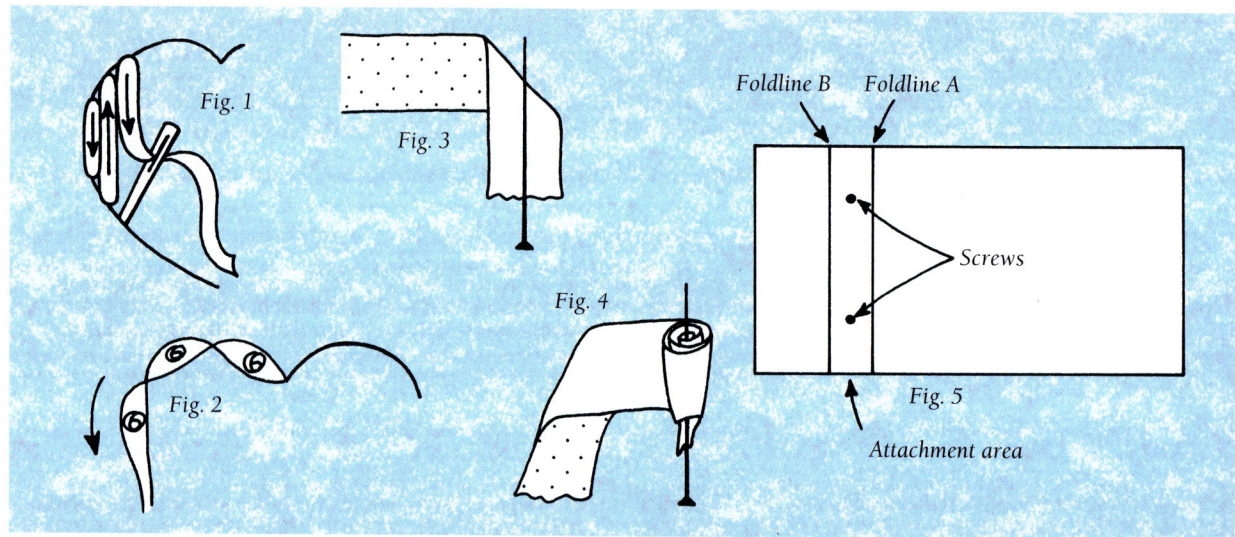

Finishing

1. Cut the length of the organza ribbon in half and, using the craft glue, attach it to the centre of the inside front and back covers of the opening edge to make a ribbon tie. Cut the raw edge of the ribbon on the diagonal and finish the ends with fray stopper.

2. Run a line of the craft glue around the edges of the wrong side of the lining and around the centre and place the lining on the inside covers of the album, pressing firmly for a short time to hold it in place.

3. To cover the centre binding, turn it to the wrong side. This covering should be kept as thin as possible, and so will not require any Pellon or Rayfelt.

4. Lightly spray the white side of the centre binding with glue and cover it with a piece of the batiste, smoothing any lumps from the centre out to the edge. Repeat for the other side.

5. Trim away any excess fabric back to the edge of the binding and cut away any of the fabric which covers the screw holes. Finish all raw edges with fray stopper.

6. Reassemble the photograph album and tie a beautiful bow with the ribbon to close the album.

Template

Embroidery Design

- Leaf
- French knot
- Pink rose
- Pale pink rose

Ribbon Flower Bouquet

MADE BY THERESE TURLEY

Deep black velvet combined with delicate ribbon flowers make this delightful little picture.

Materials

- 23 cm (9 in) square of black velveteen
- 50 cm (20 in) of 7 mm ($5/16$ in) wide silk ribbon, Pink
- 35 cm (14 in) of 15 mm (1 in) wide organza ribbon, Purple
- 20 cm (4 in) of 12 mm ($5/8$ in) wide rayon ribbon: Dark Green, Olive Green
- 35 cm (14 in) of 1 cm ($3/8$ in) wide satin ribbon, Burgundy
- 15 cm (6 in) of 2 cm ($3/4$ in) wide graduated wired ribbon, Pink to Plum
- stranded cotton, Green
- twelve to fifteen tiny pearls
- small dark beads
- thin beading needle
- pencil

Method

See the Embroidery Design on this page.
Fold the velveteen into quarters to find the centre. Mark the centre with a thread – this is where the bottom of the bouquet will sit.

For the gathered rose

1 Make four gathered roses, two using 13 cm (5 in) of Pink silk ribbon and two using 15 cm (6 in) of Burgundy ribbon. Begin by folding down one end of the ribbon at an angle of forty-five degrees to extend 1 cm ($3/8$ in).

2 Roll the ribbon over four times and take a small tuck at the bottom, then secure with a stitch. Gather along the long edge, curving the stitches up to the opposite side of the ribbon at the end (Fig. 1). Pull up the gathers tightly and wrap the gathered ribbon around the centre of the rose (Fig. 2). Secure the ribbon to the centre of the flower with small stitches.

For the organza rose (make 2)

1 Fold 16 cm ($6^{1}/4$ in) of the Purple organza ribbon in half, lengthwise, with long edges aligned. Fold down the end of the ribbon at an angle of forty-five degrees. Roll the ribbon over three times, then secure with a stitch.

2 Make small pleats in the ribbon. Roll the pleated ribbon around the rose, securing it to the centre as you go. When the ribbon is used up, tuck the end under and secure. Trim any excess ribbon. Fluff out the petals slightly to make them stand out. Make two.

For the variegated rose

1 Use 13 cm ($5^{1}/8$ in) of the variegated ribbon and 8 cm ($3^{1}/8$ in) of matching silk ribbon for the centre. Remove the wire from the darkest edge of the variegated ribbon. Using the pencil, mark every 2 cm ($3/4$ in) on one edge, then mark the same intervals on the opposite edge to make a zigzag pattern. Sew running stitches to define the zigzag (Fig. 3).

2 Gather the ribbon up into a flat circle – with the darkest shade in the centre. You should have five petals (Fig. 4). Secure the gathering.

3 Make a small silk rose with complementary silk ribbon and secure it to the centre of the flower.

For the buds

1 Make three buds, using 5 cm (2 in) each of the Green rayon ribbon and the Pink silk ribbon for each bud. To make a bud, lay the Pink ribbon on top of the Green ribbon and treat them as a single piece, varying the position of the Pink ribbon (up or down) to vary the growth of the bud.

2 Lay one end of the ribbons over the other end, pinching them together to form the base of the bud. Pull the top part of the bud up to a point. Secure the base of the bud by winding thread around it, then stitch through the base, ending with a knot (Fig. 5).

For the leaves

There are two different kinds of leaves.

1 The first type uses 5 cm (2 in) of the Green rayon ribbon and is made in the same way as the bud. Make three.

2 The second type is made using 8 cm ($3^{1}/_{8}$ in) of the lighter Green ribbon. Fold the ribbon in half, lengthwise. Gather down one side, and pull up the gathering. Pinch the raw ends and wrap thread around the base to secure it (Figs 6-8). Make two.

Assembling

1 Arrange all the flowers, buds and leaves into an attractive bouquet, then stitch them onto the background fabric.

2 Using the beading needle, attach six or seven beads and the pearls, following the diagram on page 40.

3 Using six strands of Green cotton, stitch the stems with five long uneven straight stitches, starting from under a flower.

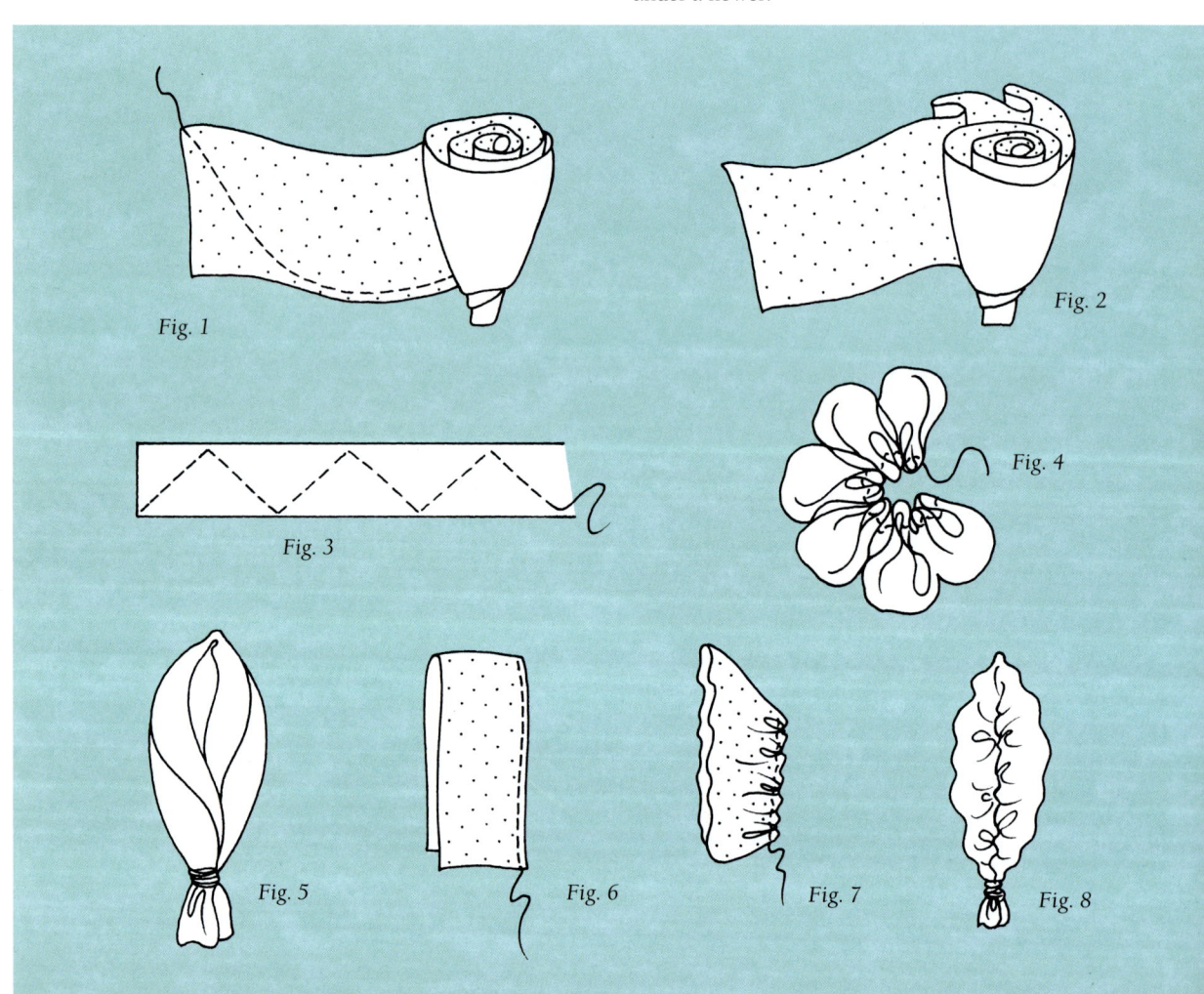

Fig. 1
Fig. 2
Fig. 3
Fig. 4
Fig. 5
Fig. 6
Fig. 7
Fig. 8

Silk Pillows

Made by Gloria McKinnon

These sumptuous little pillows can be used for brooches, hat pins, sewing pins or just as a wonderful decoration for your dressing table.

Materials

For each pillow
- 20 cm x 25 cm (8 in x 10 in) of Dupion silk
- polyester fibre fill
- stuffing tool

For the roses and lace pillow
- 2 m (2¼ yd) each of 12 mm (½ in) wide overdyed silk bias ribbon: Pink/Green, Dusty Pink, Autumn Pink
- 50 cm (20 in) each of 12 mm (½ in) wide overdyed silk bias ribbon, two Greens
- two guipure lace motifs
- Piecemakers crewel needle, size 9
- neutral sewing thread

For the rose spray pillow
- seven flocked rose leaves
- 2 m (2¼ yd) of 4 cm (1½ in) wide overdyed silk bias ribbon, Dusty Pink
- 1.5 m (1⅔ yd) of 4 mm (3/16 in) wide silk ribbon, Pale Pink

For the buttons and lace pillow
- 50 cm (20 in) of 7.5 cm (3 in) wide cream guipure lace
- 1 m (1⅛ yd) of 4 cm (1½ in) wide vintage silk ribbon, Dusty Rose
- 50 cm (20 in) of 4 cm (1½ in) wide vintage silk ribbon, Green
- Perle No. 5 thread, 739
- craft glue
- 'antique' mother-of-pearl buttons in various sizes
- two brass hearts
- 1 m (1⅛ yd) of 4 mm (3/16 in) wide silk ribbon, Cream
- neutral sewing thread
- long straw needle

Method

For all three pillows

1 Fold the Dupion silk over double so that it measures 12.5 cm x 20 cm (5 in x 8 in). Sew around three sides with a small machine stitch. To keep the corners square, stitch as shown in figure 1. Turn the piece right side out, making sure all the corners are pushed out completely.

2 Stuff the pillow very, very firmly. When you think it is properly stuffed, use the stuffing tool to push more stuffing down the sides and into the corners. This will ensure your pillow remains firm. Close the open side of the pillow with a ladder stitch.

Roses and lace pillow

1 To take the whiteness out of the lace motifs, dye them in a little strawberry tea.

2 Tie a neat knot approximately 2.5 cm (1 in) from the end of the ribbon (Fig. 2).

3 Holding the short end against the long end, tie off the top by winding thread around, just below the knot. This forms the centre of the rose (Fig. 3).

4 Fold back the top edge of the ribbon and begin rolling and folding until you have a pleasing rose-like shape. With each full turn, stitch through the base to hold the rose securely (Fig. 4). When the rose is completed, cut the ribbon and secure the last roll with stitching, leaving a long thread for attaching the rose. Make at least twelve roses.

For the rose buds

1. Fold the short end of a piece of Pink silk ribbon as shown in figure 5. Fold the other end over as shown in figure 6, then tie off the ribbon by winding around with thread.

2. Wrap the bud with Green ribbon and catch it securely at the base. Make at least six buds in this way.

For the leaves

Make five leaves in the same way as the rose buds, omitting the final step.

Finishing

Centre then stitch the lace motifs onto the top of the pillow. Pin the roses, leaves and rose buds around the motifs. When you are pleased with the arrangement, sew the leaves and buds on first, then attach the roses, working from the edge to the centre.

Rose spray pillow

1. Make two roses in the same way as the roses on the Roses and Lace pillow.

2. Arrange the leaves on the pillow, using pins to hold them in position. Place the roses amongst the leaves, then stitch the leaves to the pillow, using the sewing thread.

3. Cut the silk ribbon in half and fold it into loops and tails. Stitch the ribbon under the roses, then stitch the roses into place. You may need to catch the petals into place with a couple of small stitches.

Buttons and lace pillow

1. Cut the lace into two lengths which will fit around the pillow, following the shape of the motifs in the lace. Stitch the lace to the pillow, covering it completely and having the ends of the lace meet on the back of the pillow.

2. Make one rose, two buds and one leaf, following the directions given for the Roses and Lace Pillow. Stitch them to the top of the pillow, using the long needle.

3. Using the Perle thread, stitch through the buttons, tying off the thread at the back. Glue the buttons into position around the rose.

4. Thread the silk ribbon between the fabric of the pillow and the lace up to the side of the rose. Attach it to the rose with tiny stitches. Thread a heart, then tie a bow. Trim the ribbon ends. Attach the second heart to the other side of the rose.

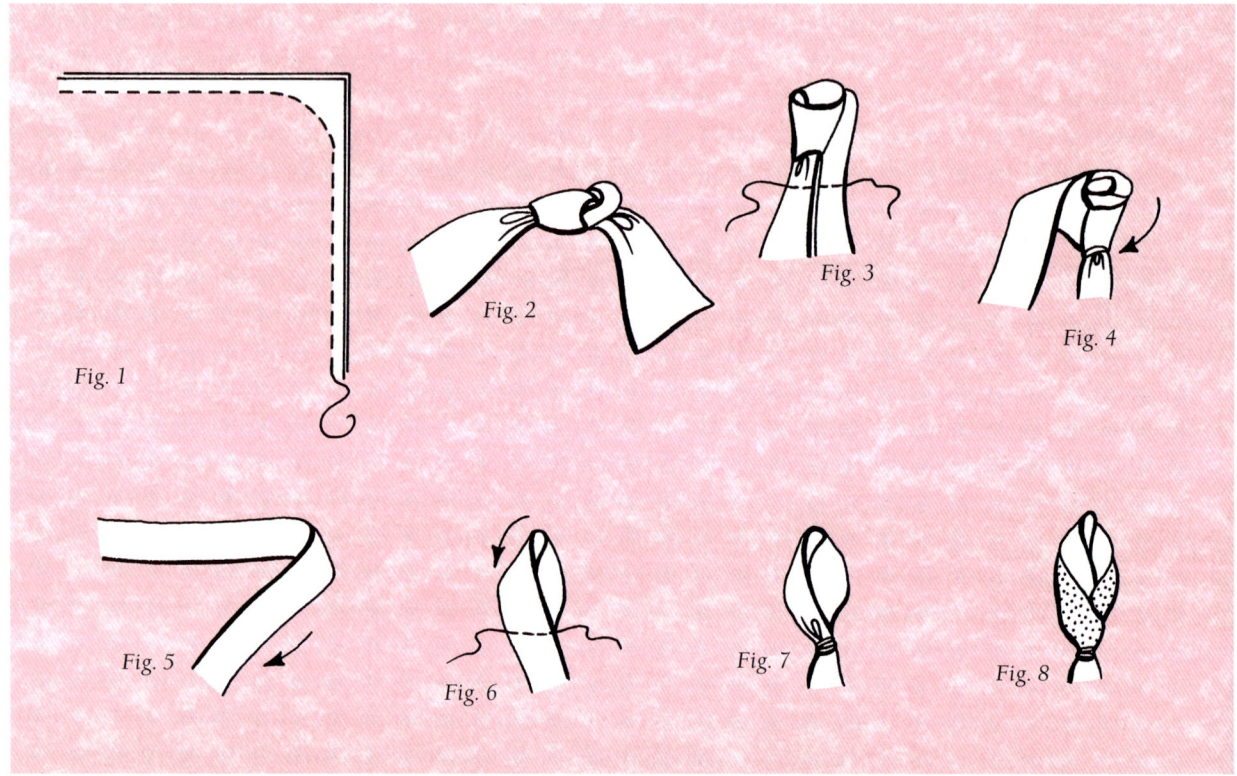

Fig. 1
Fig. 2
Fig. 3
Fig. 4
Fig. 5
Fig. 6
Fig. 7
Fig. 8

Porcelain Box

EMBROIDERED BY KATHY AWENDER

Show off your silk ribbon embroidery talents by mounting your work on this lovely porcelain box.

Materials

- porcelain box kit with a 10 cm (4 in) diameter lid
- 20 cm (8 in) square of white linen fabric
- 46 cm (18 in) each of 7 mm ($^5/_{16}$ in) wide silk ribbon: Light Pink, Dark Pink, Purple, Light Green
- 92 cm (36 in) each of 4 mm ($^3/_{16}$ in) wide silk ribbon: Medium Green, Dark Green, Pink, Yellow
- Kanagawa silk thread, Green
- tracing paper
- pencil
- water-soluble marker pen
- cardboard
- wadding
- embroidery hoop
- Piecemakers tapestry needle, size 22
- strong sewing thread
- craft glue

Method

See the Embroidery Design on page 48.

Preparation

1. Trace and cut out a circle of cardboard and one of wadding, using the template provided with the kit.

2. Trace the circle onto the centre of the fabric square. The embroidery will be centred in this circle.

Embroidery

1. Trace the embroidery design, using the marker pen or simply indicate the main features with dots.

2. Secure the fabric in the embroidery hoop and work the embroidery following the design and the key.

Finishing

1. Cut out the embroidery 2.5 cm (1 in) away from the traced line. Using the strong sewing thread, sew small running stitches close to the cut edge.

2. Lay the embroidery face down with the wadding circle centred on top. Place a few drops of glue on the edge of the cardboard circle, then place it over the wadding. Pull up the gathering tightly, securing the wadding and the cardboard. Tie the ends firmly.

3. Set the embroidery into the frame provided and complete the box following the instruction given with the kit.

Embroidery Design

Straight stitch leaves in 4 mm (3/16 in) wide Medium Green

Feather stitch in Green silk thread
French knots in 4 mm (3/16 in) wide Pink

Fly stitch iris in 7 mm (5/16 in) wide Purple
Straight stitch stem in Green silk thread
Twisted straight stitch leaves in 7 mm (5/16 in) wide Light Green

Loop stitch (2 rows) with colonial knot centre in 7 mm (5/16 in) Light Pink

Back stitch in 7 mm (5/16 in) Dark Pink

Straight stitch bud in 7 mm (5/16 in) Dark Pink
Fly stitch calyx in 4 mm (3/16 in) Medium Green
Straight stitch stem in Green silk thread

Ribbon stitch leaf in 7 mm (5/16 in) Light Green

French knots in 4 mm (3/16 in) Yellow